MW01504241

A Tale of Water

Poetry by Sandra Marshburn

Published by Prolific Press Inc.

It is with gratitude that the author would like to thank the following publications in which these poems first appeared: *Common Ground*: "January Walk": *Kakalak*: "A Tale of Water"; *Surrounded, Living with Islands* anthology: "Barrier Island"; *Snail Mail Review*: "Subtract"; *Third Wednesday*: "It woke me before dawn"; *Timber Creek Review*: "Low Tide"; *Toledo Review* and *Telling Time* chapbook: "Time on My Hands"; *Second Wind*: "Wetland"; *Kerf* and *Telling Time* chapbook: "Inland Thoughts during Hurricane Season"; *The Longleaf Pine*: "Driving Here to There"; *The Poetry Society of South Carolina 2019 Yearbook*: "Descendants"; *Tar River Poetry* and *Telling Time* and *Winter Beach* chapbooks: "Perennial Bed"; *Undertow* chapbook: "A Dream of Middle Years".

A Tale of Water
©2019 Sandra Marshburn
Published by Prolific Press Inc., Johnstown, PA (USA)
Printed in the USA by Prolific Press Inc. Johnstown, PA (USA)
ISBN: 978-1-63275-186-7
Cover Image licensed by Ingram Images
Edited by: Glenn Lyvers
Assistant editor: April Zipser

Quality Guarantee: Many of the books published by Prolific Press Inc. are printed in-house and finished by hand, using papers and inks that surpass marketplace standards. Generally, this means better quality, but with any handmade product, there is always the possibility of error. If you are unsatisfied with the quality of this product, in its binding or general manufacture, please contact Prolific Press Inc. for a free replacement.

For Cassie,
who introduced her parents to Edisto.

Contents...

Barrier Island

On a road map, let your finger trace
South Carolina Highway 174 East and run it
across the Intracoastal Waterway Bridge.
Then drive your finger down the center
of Edisto Island to the Atlantic Ocean.
Dip your finger into map blue water
that runs a circle from river to ocean to river.

Drive the real road to water and sift
your fingers through sand to find sea
creatures' teeth and vertebrae.
Look for a live oak bent to the ground
by the 1893 hurricane, and see how
it grew new trunks upright.

Walk to the mound Edisto Indians
made of discarded oyster shells.
See fields of tomatoes, beans, corn, melons,
no more rice, no more cotton.
Take a name from the phone book and trace it
to an African slave. Trace the same name
to an English planter. Know that
descendants of both live here.

Consult a tide chart from the grocery.
Chase ghost crabs and your dog
away from sea turtle nests.
Spot a bald eagle, painted bunting.
Do not ask when drinking water will be
improved. Do not ask for fast food or hotels.

In season, obey local officials who knock
on your door and tell you to evacuate.
The causeway will flood, high bridge
will be closed due to wind. If you don't go,
wear your name on a wristband.

It Woke Me Before Dawn

the siren I could hear traveling for three miles
before a rescue truck whizzed by
on the highway. Fire truck screaming
after it. Small town on the eastern tip
of an island, any emergency is likely
to be about someone I know
or the only grocery burning.
You can call the 24-hour gas station
to ask what's going on, but
they sometimes make it up.

When it was quiet again, I heard
whippoorwills call. Tried to re-
enter my last dream about a man
cutting down oleander bushes
with a chain saw. I yelled at him to stop,
and I couldn't find my phone.
Birds circled above, nests lost.

Along the Way

Boxer dog at the shoreline steps
into water, moves back, steps in,
out again, then shakes it off.

Baby straddling mother's hip
twists his head away from land
and stares at waves coming

and going, eyelids starting
to flutter. At 7 am, young man walks
on a dirt road east, then west

never meeting your eyes.
Old man sits in the back of
his pickup at a rural three-way

intersection. Before you look
both ways, look for him
with his smile and handmade sign
that asks if you are saved.

Low Tide

Out with my retriever for a July sunrise,
I searched rocks and jetty exposed by low tide
for sea anemone, a name to roll around

on lips and tongue. They wave stinging
tentacles that look like flower petals,
small shrimp among their prey. No waving
that morning, only dark cylinder bodies

camouflaged on granite rock. When I
touched one, it felt like a dog's leathery
nose, wanting moisture. Which made me

turn to my companion who ran back
and forth from wave line to dry sand
sniffing ghost crab holes and clumps

of seaweed, measuring new
territory we had been granted.
Tidal clock ticking, the anemone
waited for the sea to cover them.

Inland Thoughts During Hurricane Season

Walk the shore and count them
as you climb over, jetties
thrust into the ocean

to break waves, to save sand, sea oats
and beach: granite and wood rough on your feet,
the sun-baked smell of creosote

oozing from timbers. Look to a horizon
so distant it appears to curve.
On jetty after jetty
out beyond the STAY OFF signs,
sunbathers and terns perch together on the rocks,
moss and barnacle

exposed by low tide. On the bluest days,
a man in a bikini mimed a Charles Atlas pose—
perhaps for someone

or anyone while the sea lapped the wall
murmuring its indifference
to whatever we do.

Crossing the Dawhoo River

It took years on the island to make me
feel I belong here, to understand others when
they say they are uneasy off the island,
anxious to cross the bridge and get home.
The new bridge replaced a drawbridge,
still rendered by local artists.

Seen from a boat underneath
the concrete bridge brings you up
and eases you down onto land going
in either direction, as if someone designed it
knowing that traveling away or back
calls for a gentle transition.

On a nest atop an old power pole,
where the highway turns into a bridge
and vice versa, an osprey often observes
our travels. When we are told to evacuate,

there's only one way, two lanes going
the same direction. We wait, impatient
for an "all clear" from authorities or
from ourselves. Emboldened
by the smooth transition to the island

I return to the work ahead.
Sun high, an ocean whose anger is spent,
I am back where I belong.

A Tale of Water

After the girl's father died, just as he
had told her to, she continued to walk
every day to the road's end and look at
a great lake, the lake he loved.
It offered red sunsets, a hint of Chicago
lights after dark, fog and a foghorn,
the diaphone kind. Her father had lived
before zebra mussels imported
in ships' ballast tanks disturbed
the lake's native food chain.

When the girl moved south to mountains,
she lived beside a river, inferior in her mind
to a great lake, her father had never
mentioned rivers, but she liked seeing
the other side. Woods over there, a fox,
scaly sycamore trunks, railroad tracks.
Once in a while, the river sported
orange booms around patches of water
to contain an oil spill. No one admitted
where the oil came from.

Older, she lives by an ocean where
water never ends. She keeps track of tides,
grew to like a salty taste and smell.
Thinks of her father as she walks there
every day, summer water rising
to 86 degrees, too much carbon
dioxide, fish dying for oxygen,
coral reefs diminished by
chemicals--these bodies of water
her granddaughters' burden.

Driving Here to There

For a 10 am appointment
leafless trees filtering light
I saw a brown suit jacket

buttoned up on a hanger
sway from a branch. No time
to go back and look again.

I passed a closed tavern, chairs
upended in the yard, this
is rural. A big funeral

not far from here by the time
I return. Black suits preferred.
Several miles farther, a tree

trunk dressed in bra and hula
skirt, fabulous colors on
grey bark. You have to know

where to look. Over the bridge
four lane highways, then
stoplights measure the final blocks.

Today I dressed with care. Those
waiting for me will have no patience
with tales of clothes on trees.

Peterson Says the Name Alone Describes Them

No one else there. Mosquitoes
hummed in our ears. Minnows
jumped and fell so fast
we could only hear them.
Periwinkles clung to spartina.

Downstream thirty feet, two roseate
spoonbills wading. Light pink juveniles.
We held our breath. Swinging their heads
side to side, they ignored us, stirring
marsh soup with their spoons.

Ghostly white, high on live
oak branch, an egret eyed us,
as if to say, nothing they needed
from us, time to go. Ashamed of our
noisy truck, we drove away.

Descendants

Word got out that a famous museum
was coming to dismantle and pack up the last
Edisto Island slave cabin. It stood but barely
on land where Europeans first settled.
Descendants of slaves on the island
began naming their ancestors who had lived
in the cabin before the Civil War
and as freedmen into the 20th century.

When she lived there as a young girl,
one woman told how Black Angus cows
stuck their heads in the door. Others talked
about two rooms, a loft, chimney fires.

They arrived the day it came down,
board after board numbered, hand-forged nails
collected, one descendant photographed looking
out a window frame before the wall was taken,
his expression hard to read.

As the day wore on, a woman sang herself
into the spirit of her great-grandmother.
While pieces were loaded onto trucks,
people surprised themselves with tears.

Ground the cabin had covered gave up
evidence of lives there: coin, button,
pottery sherd, animal bone. We hear
about the restoration and wait for the cabin's
placement in public halls some will visit
and some will not. Marked by a palmetto
near the bluff above the North Edisto River,
we know where it stood.

A Dream of Middle Years

Windows overlooked the ocean
and a fireplace burned brightly
in the house I dreamed, built of stone,
unlike any I know.
When I tried to reach the shore,
the house became a maze:
every door opened into another room.

Left by strangers, quilts and vases
were the same ones I remembered
from my mother's bedroom. Already late
for something, I hurried to string
tiny beads on my daughter's necklace.
When I woke, many were left unstrung
and waves splashed against the windows.

Perennial Bed

Summers I weeded a bed of perennials
that fronted our house. And listened
to my mother lament the pocked
cement step eaten by salt
spread against winter ice.

I heard her explain to anyone how
paint peeled from the shingles, wood
not properly seasoned, the house
built during World War II.

On a southern coast, now I plant
waxy-leafed evergreens impervious
to salt spray. Only certain plants survive
with tricks like spikes and tendrils
to attach themselves or leaves
narrow as knife blades that conserve
moisture under a relentless sun.

Inside, on an afternoon cooled by
reaching arms of live oak, it was
the perennial bed of forty years ago
I dreamed of. On twelve-year-old knees,
I weeded the bed, errant plants seeming
to grow back as I pulled them out,
rough cement a reminder of seasons
to come, salt leaving its bitter mark.

After sun falls behind banked
western clouds, I carry water
to yucca and bayberry
tenuously holding on.

National Estuary Day

DNR pontoon boat loaded with old people
who volunteer. This ride was payback.
Estuary, Latin for tide, surge, heat,
we were in the middle of it. This one
carries the flow from ACE Basin rivers:
Ashepoo, Combahee and Edisto
into St. Helena Sound, all smooth on the tongue.

Marine science students talked to us, dragged a net
for 15 minutes, then the strong ones hauled it in.
Some specimens were placed in jars of estuary water
and passed around. Others held up to show us
a mouth, a spot, forked tail, compound eyes.
They told us about species, sex, health, how
they live, how they die. A horseshoe crab went
hand to hand, smelling salty, so we could see
the gills and learn that its tail exists only
to flip the crab over when stranded on its back.

A sunny day, high tide, we talked about salinity,
oxygen in the water, presence of diverse species.
Right there, right then, they told us it's ok,
this water is ok to support these life forms.
A gift to us. Right there, right then.

Living on an Island

Driving home, she says,
this is an island. The arching bridge
delivers her to the only main road

there is, two lanes through marsh
to ocean, plenty of side roads dirt
and dead end. Some day she will be

surprised by something
that makes it impossible for her
to stay. She will move to a town

busy with intersections and strangers.
Here she nods to everyone.
She has seen them all at the grocery.

She will leave keeping the island
every night in her dreams. Every day
she will be ready to go there.

January Walk

Fallen stars tossed out by cold waves lie dead
among shells and seaweed. You count a dozen
of them, five stiff arms showing grey backs
or white undersides and look around to see who
you will have to share them with. Not the guy
with the metal detector. There's no one else.
Seven is enough; you leave the ones with tips of legs
nipped off. Hurrying home as if they are forbidden,

you finger spiny skin in your coat pockets.
They smell of salt and fish in the warm
kitchen. On the counter, you arrange them,
already liking them more than a quilted star
hung to hide the breaker box, more
than a star-shaped, frosted paperweight.

Subtract

Take away engines in the harbor.
Refuse the laugh of gulls.
Walk toward sand, then

far from bathers who splash.
Keep the soundless dive
of pelicans and egrets

motionless in the marsh.
At low tide wind whispers
to your hair. Sit down

in damp sand, the roll of
small waves slower than
your pulse. Imagine water

a mirror and hold your breath.

Coming Home After Dark

Headlights approaching are few—
time to return, not leave.

Among trees, windows lit
in houses not visible by day,
people already home.

Your eyes appreciate reflectors
that edge the road.

After you cross the only bridge
to the island, the road
you know by heart

becomes hazardous.
Whatever drew you away
now seems not worth the trip back.

Two deer stand on the shoulder
while you pray they stay there.

On this clear night, magnified
constellations give some comfort.

Twenty minutes from bridge
to your door, you follow
one car's taillights the whole way.

For the last two miles, familiar
businesses now closed, the soft rush

of rhythmic waves and yard lights
lead to your driveway where you
are welcomed by your barking dog.

Time on My Hands

Thirty years at the same job and soon
I'll be done with that. Words I no longer
need will be replaced with names

of shore birds and waders. I'll patrol
the early morning beach in search
of turtle tracks. And measure time

by walking until the evening sun
touches water, and when it does, turn
for home. There will be time to make beds

of day lilies, trim the rosemary bush,
decide which clothes I'll never wear again.
But what will I do when hands

won't plant, legs won't walk? Will I
grow still like my great uncle who sat
for hours in his chair by the window

reading a few pages, rising occasionally
to look at his pocket watch, then
out the window to see if rain

was coming, if grass had grown,
if time had passed. He'd sit down again, hold
one hand in the other and close his eyes.

Wetland

At high tide, earth loses form.
When marsh swells to lake,
dolphin and osprey dive,
a swarming mix

of fresh water and salt.
After low tide drains the basin,
some Midwesterner might mistake
sweet grass waving

for wheat fields. Leggy egret
and ibis wade the marsh's
soft belly, moon already turned
toward flood.

Summer shimmers on one solid line
of blacktop that runs through. Roll
down the windows and smell creation's
warm brine,

the way it must have been in
the beginning: blessed creatures
of water and air, with all of us
still to come.

State Route 174 as Muse

> "The road out of Edisto is the best I know
> to drive with nothing, or a lot, on your mind."
> *Edisto Revisited* by Padgett Powell

I drive it and trace words on sweating windows,
the road beneath oak live with moss
as seductive as a canopied bed.
A road that breaks wide into sky
and marsh where a wood stork's foot
stirs up dinner. At high tide
when marsh creeps onto berm
syllables flood my tongue. No place

to turn around, the bridge sweeps me
over the Dawhoo River and down
to landscapes inland and ordinary.
At the first stop sign it's over,
all words dried from glass,
forbidden off the island.

Prolific Press Inc.
Johnstown, PA